PETER WAITZMAN

Living The Dream

5 Strategies That Changed My Life

This book was professionally typeset on Reedsy.
Find out more at reedsy.com

Contents

1

Living The Dream?

The Grind

The fluorescent lights flickered overhead as I stared at my reflection in the darkened office window. It was 3 AM, and downtown Chicago below had long since gone to sleep. My coffee—the fifth cup of the night—had gone cold, but I took another sip anyway. Behind me, three monitors glowed with endless lines of code, a labyrinth of problems I needed to solve before the sun rose.

"Living the dream, baby," I whispered to my reflection, watching as the corners of my mouth twisted into what had become my signature sardonic smile. The phrase had started as an inside joke, a shield against the crushing weight of reality. Now, it was my battle cry, my defense mechanism, my daily lie.

The truth? I was twenty-three, making a decent salary, and completely miserable. By society's standards, I had "made it." I was living in the hot Bucktown neighborhood, driving a BMW, and spending long weekends skiing. I was living what everyone told me was "the dream."

But dreams aren't supposed to leave you hollow. They're not supposed to have you calculating how many hours of sleep you can sacrifice before your body gives out. They're not supposed to turn you into someone who measures their worth by the number of successful on-time software launches.

I remember the exact moment everything changed. It wasn't during a grand epiphany or a dramatic breakdown. It was on a regular Tuesday morning as I mumbled my usual "living the dream" response to a concerned coworker. She didn't laugh. I didn't laugh. The joke had long stopped being funny, and I realized I was in need of some help.

There I was, young and theoretically in my prime, treating my life like an endurance test I had to survive rather than an adventure I got to live. The most ironic part? I told myself I was doing all this to build a better life—but I was too busy grinding to actually live. My principles, my dreams, my very identity were luxuries I thought I couldn't afford. "Principles belong to those who can afford them," I'd say with a shrug as if accepting misery was somehow noble.

That night marked the beginning of my awakening. Not because I suddenly figured everything out but because I finally admitted I needed to find a better way forward. The path from that fluorescent-lit epiphany to early retirement at forty-two wasn't straight or simple, but it started with one crucial realization: The life I was living wasn't a dream—it was a hamster wheel. And it was time to wake up.

Why Listen to a Regular Joe?

Now, I know what you're thinking. "Who is this guy, and why should I care about his advice?" Fair question! I'm not some Silicon Valley wunderkind or a Wall Street mogul. I'm just an average Joe from the Midwest who stumbled upon a few life-changing strategies that turned my world upside down (in the best way possible).

I was a typical college graduate drowning in debt, desperately treading water in the vast ocean of corporate America. That was me. I was caught in the classic work-money-fun conundrum. You know the one:

1. Need money for fun stuff
2. Work more hours to get money
3. No time left for fun stuff
4. Repeat until you're too old to enjoy anything

Sound familiar? But here's the remarkable part. I managed to break free from this vicious cycle and retire at 42. Yes, you read that right. Forty-two! And no, I didn't win the lottery or inherit anything from a long-lost uncle. I didn't do it by moving off the grid or taking everything to the extreme. I did it while living life. I collected the cars of my dreams, took unreal vacations with my family, and pursued every passion project on my bucket list. And it all happened because I stumbled upon the power of small, strategic changes.

The Domino Effect

I always thought that life-changing moments would be big, momentous occasions that were easily recognizable and justifiably celebrated. I thought the moments that mattered were when the obscure actor gets cast in the blockbuster movie, or you're ringing the bell at the stock exchange on the day your company goes public. I never expected it to be the small change you make to your routine or the simple tool you embrace for a few minutes a day. Well, that's exactly how life-changing transformations work. One small change can set off a chain reaction that leads to incredible results.

My journey was like rolling a snowball down a hill. It started small, but as it gained momentum, it grew bigger and bigger, eventually dragging me along for the ride. Before I knew it, I had achieved financial independence and was waving goodbye to my corporate cubicle. It was like waking up from a long, tedious dream and realizing that life could be so much more.

The Five Game-Changing Strategies

Now, I know what you're saying, "Okay, so, what's this amazing secret recipe?" Well, I'm about to walk you through the five strategies that turned my life around. And the best part? They're not some exclusive, members-only club type of deals. These are strategies that anyone — yes, even pantless remote workers — can implement.

Here's a sneak peek:

1. The "Becoming Perfect" Strategy
2. The "Easy Money" Method
3. The "Waste Not" Technique
4. The "Cheat Code" Approach
5. The "Time Recovery" System

Now, I won't go into detail about each strategy here (that's what the rest of the book is for), but I promise you this: These aren't your run-of-the-mill "wake up at 5 am and eat kale" type of tips. I tried kale once and will never do it again. These are practical, actionable strategies that don't require you to have a million Instagram followers or the charisma of James Bond.

Nope, all you need is the willingness to try something new and the patience to let the snowball effect work its magic.

Your Results Will Definitely Vary

Now, I'm not promising that you'll be able to leave your job like I did. Your journey might look different. Maybe you'll use these strategies to start that passion project you've been dreaming about. Or perhaps you'll finally have the time and resources to travel the world. The beauty of these strategies is that they're flexible and adaptable to your unique goals and circumstances.

Think of it like a choose-your-own-adventure book, but instead of facing dragons or exploring haunted houses, you're navigating the challenges of adult life and coming out on top.

What It Really Looks Like

Fast forward to today, and "living the dream" has taken on a whole new meaning for me. Let me paint you a picture of what my average day looks like now:

- I wake up naturally. No alarm clock is needed. Why? Because I'm excited about the day ahead. (Also, because I switched to an incredible memory foam mattress with a cooling gel layer.)

- My mornings are mine. Thanks to my newfound productivity skills, I can afford to start my day with some me-time.
- Work is no longer a chore but a choice. I focus on projects that excite me, knowing that my diversified income streams mean I'm not dependent on any single source.
- My time is my own. I've learned to say no to things that don't align with my goals, which means I have more time for the things that do.
- Financial stress? I'm not sure that it ever goes away completely, but thanks to my new approach to debt and my multiple income streams, I know that I have more than enough coming in.
- I'm constantly growing. Whether it's learning a new skill, exploring a new business idea, or just reading up on the latest in my field, I'm always pushing myself to scale up and think bigger.

Now, when someone asks me how I'm doing, and I say, "Living the dream," I mean it. And the best part? I'm not special. I'm not a genius or a trust fund baby. I'm just a regular person who figured out a few key strategies and applied them consistently.

Your Turn

So, are you ready to turn that sarcastic "living the dream" into a genuine statement of contentment? Fantastic! Remember, this journey isn't always going to be smooth sailing. There will be days when you wonder, "Is this really doing anything?" That's when consistency becomes your best friend. Stay the course, keep putting one foot in front of the other, and trust the process.

So, let's dive into the roadmap from sarcastic quips to genuine contentment. Most of it is shockingly simple - so much so that you'll be frustrated that you didn't start it earlier. And if you embrace it, I'm telling you that it can change everything. Remember, every great story has a beginning. This is yours. So take that first small step to truly "living the dream."

2

Becoming Perfect

The Productivity Puzzle

The steering wheel of my car was not designed to be a file folder. Yet there I was, wedging a crumpled proposal into the leather circle like some desperate backyard mechanic. It had come to this: literally embedding my work into my vehicle because my brain—this supposedly sophisticated organ capable of complex problem-solving—couldn't accomplish the simple task of remembering to bring a document to the office.

The paper crackled as I adjusted it, making sure it wouldn't fall during my morning commute. I couldn't help but laugh at the absurdity of the situation. Here I was, a professional who prided himself on being tech-savvy and productivity-minded, reduced to turning my car into a mobile filing cabinet.

It hadn't started this way. On Sunday evening, I'd been the picture of responsibility, deliberately placing the proposal on my kitchen counter where I couldn't possibly miss it. "There," I'd thought confidently, "I'm all set for tomorrow."

Monday morning, I was the normal zombie idiot who walked right past that proposal without a second glance.

"No big deal," I reassured myself as I discovered its absence at the office.

"I'll just grab it tomorrow." But Tuesday morning brought the same result—the proposal sat untouched on my counter, probably developing a sense of abandonment issues by now.

By Wednesday, what had started as a minor inconvenience was morphing into a genuine problem. The proposal needed to be submitted by Friday, and somehow, this simple task—literally picking up a piece of paper and moving it from Point A to Point B—had become my personal Everest.

The irony wasn't lost on me. I could manage complex projects, meet critical deadlines, and juggle multiple responsibilities. I had calendars, reminders, and to-do lists coming out of my ears. Yet here I was, being repeatedly defeated by a single folder sitting on my counter.

That's when it hit me. If I, someone who actively sought out productivity tools and embraced technology, could be so thoroughly stymied by such a basic task, something fundamental was missing in how we approach organization and productivity.

This wasn't just about a forgotten proposal. It was about the gap between our brain's incredible capabilities and its frustrating limitations. It was about the disconnect between having systems for big things while still dropping the ball on small ones. And most importantly, it was about finding a better way to manage the countless details that make up our increasingly complex lives.

As I embarked on a quest to bridge this gap—to understand how someone could accomplish big things while maintaining consistency in small tasks—I discovered a system that would change my life forever.

In our quest for self-improvement, we often strive for perfection. I'm pretty sure that true perfection is unattainable (otherwise, I might obsess about my occasional flaws). However, the journey toward it can lead to remarkable growth and efficiency. Enter the Getting Things Done (GTD) system - a powerful tool that propels us closer to the ideal of perfect productivity. As we delve into this life-changing system, remember that becoming perfect isn't about flawless execution but about continual progress and mastery of our daily lives.

Welcome to the Modern Life Juggling Act

Let's face it. We're not in the simpler times our grandparents lived in. Back then, life was more "streamlined." You had a job, you did your job, you went home. Rinse and repeat. The biggest decision of the day might have been whether to have pot roast or meatloaf for dinner.

But now? We're all unofficial circus performers, juggling a gazillion "micro-projects" in our daily lives. Work deadlines, family responsibilities, home maintenance, car repairs, grocery shopping, bill payments, taxes, community commitments - the list goes on. It's like trying to complete an escape room while being constantly hit in the face with pies.

With all this mental overload, it's no wonder something occasionally slips through the cracks. But there's a solution to this madness.

Enter the Unassuming Hero

Allow me to introduce you to the productivity system that changed my life: the Getting Things Done (GTD) system! Developed by the brilliant David Allen, this system is like a personal assistant for your brain. It's not quite Radar O'Reilly to your Colonel Blake, but it's pretty darn close.

Now, I could go on for days about the intricacies of GTD (there are multi-day conferences dedicated to it), but I'll spare you the deep dive and give you the CliffsNotes version. Think of it as *GTD: The Abridged and Customized Edition.*

The Brain Is Fantastic and Terrible

Before we jump into the nitty-gritty of GTD, let's talk about your brain for a second. It's an incredible machine. It can solve complex problems, create beautiful art, and come up with terrible jokes instantaneously. But when it comes to remembering mundane tasks? It's about as reliable as a British car.

Think of your brain as a super-advanced computer. It's got an amazing processor (problem-solving skills) and data storage (memories). But unlike your laptop, which can happily chug along doing repetitive tasks without breaking a sweat, your brain gets overwhelmed trying to keep track of every little thing.

That's where GTD comes in. It's like hiring a super-efficient personal assistant for your brain, freeing it up to do what it does best: being engaged and solving problems.

Capture and Inbox

Pillar 1: Capture Everything

The first rule of GTD is to capture everything. The moment a thought pops into your head - whether it's a work task, a grocery item, or a brilliant idea for the next great American novel - write it down. Don't wait. Don't think, "Oh, I'll remember this later." Trust me, you won't. Your brain is too busy trying to remember the lyrics to that hit from the 80s, "Ooh, baby, do you know what that's worth?"

The key is to have a capture system that's always with you. It could be a notepad, your phone, or a voice recorder. Personally, I use my iPhone to email tasks to myself because it's always with me.

Pillar 2: The Almighty Inbox

Once you've captured all these thoughts and tasks, they need a place to live. This is your inbox. This is where everything goes, no matter what it is. Work stuff, personal stuff, and the Christmas card you need to order in six months all go into the inbox.

Now, I know what you're thinking. "But won't that get cluttered?" Maybe for a little while, but at least everything is captured. The secret is in the review. Set aside time regularly (I do it every morning during my "hour of power") to go through your inbox. Sort tasks into appropriate projects or categories and add due dates as needed.

Putting It All Together

By capturing everything and regularly reviewing and organizing it, you're freeing your mind from the constant worry of forgetting something. It's like having a safety net for your thoughts. This system essentially acts as a "second brain," a concept that's gained popularity in recent years. Just as your biological brain processes and stores information, this external system—your second brain—captures, organizes, and makes retrievable all the important data, tasks, and ideas in your life.

With this second brain in place, you can focus on being creative, spontaneous, and productive because you trust your system to remind you of what needs to be done. It's not about offloading your thinking but rather about creating a reliable system that complements your biological memory and cognitive processes.

Imagine walking into a meeting and impressing everyone with your preparedness. Picture yourself tackling projects with ease, never dropping the ball on deadlines. Envision a world where you remember to bring those important papers to work. That's the power of GTD and your newly developed second brain.

Not Just for Lone Wolves

Here's a little secret. GTD isn't just for individuals. It works wonders for teams too. I implemented the GTD system for my team at work. I wasn't sure what to expect, but it was like watching a group of eager workers slowly see the light. We used an online project management tool to capture tasks, assign responsibilities, and track progress. The result? A massively more organized, productive, and successful team. And yes, many teammates took the GTD philosophy and integrated it into their personal lives as well.

Your Ticket to Success

If you take nothing else from this chapter (or this book, for that matter), let it be this: adopt the GTD system and embrace the concept of a second brain. It doesn't matter if you're working a 9-to-5, running multiple businesses, or trying to organize a household of unruly kids. This system is your ticket to a whole new world of efficiency, accuracy, and peace of mind.

GTD isn't just about getting things done; it's about revolutionizing your entire approach to life. It's the foundation that allows you to achieve things you never thought possible. With GTD, you're not just managing tasks – you're opening doors to exciting opportunities that once seemed out of reach.

Imagine a life where stress melts away, where you consistently hit deadlines, and where you have the mental space to pursue your passions. That's the GTD difference. It's not about being a genius or having a photographic memory. It's about leveraging a system that handles the minutiae your brain struggles with, freeing you to focus on what truly matters.

But here's the kicker. GTD is just the beginning. Once you master this system, you'll find yourself equipped to take on more – much more. Want to crush it at work and snag that promotion? GTD's got your back. Dreaming of starting a side hustle? GTD will help you juggle it all. Yearning to improve your health, boost your finances, or simply enjoy life more? GTD is your launchpad.

So, are you ready to unleash your productivity potential, build your second brain, and embark on the journey of becoming perfect? Give GTD a try. Watch as it transforms not just your to-do list but your entire life trajectory.

Remember, becoming perfect isn't about never making mistakes – it's about having a system that catches those mistakes before someone else does. GTD continuously improves your productivity and expands your capabilities. With GTD and your second brain, you're not just dreaming of doing more and doing it better. You're actively working towards it - one captured thought and organized task at a time.

This isn't just about getting organized – it's about setting the stage for a life filled with achievement, growth, and fulfillment. GTD is your first step into a larger world, where the horizons of possibility stretch far beyond what you once thought possible. Are you ready to take that step?

3

Easy Money

Side Hustles and Financial Freedom

The menu trembled slightly in my hands as I scanned the prices for the third time, my eyes automatically filtering out anything above $8. My wife sat across from me, doing the same dance with her own menu. We'd chosen this modest local restaurant for our rare night out—a chance to escape our daily routine and pretend, just for an hour or two, that we weren't counting every penny.

"The chicken special looks good," she said softly, but I caught the slight hesitation in her voice. At $6.99, it was the cheapest entrée on the menu. I nodded, knowing we'd both end up ordering it, not because it was what we craved, but because spending an extra two or three dollars felt like an impossible luxury.

We sat there with our ice waters—no sodas, no appetizers—in a restaurant filled with the gentle clink of wine glasses and the casual ordering from other diners requesting exactly what they wanted. The contrast was stark. It wasn't that we couldn't afford to be there at all; we'd budgeted carefully for this modest dinner out. But the freedom to choose any item on the menu? That felt like a fantasy.

That's when it hit me, right there between the breadsticks and the forced smiles: How had we arrived at a place where a few dollars could dictate our choices so completely? Not hundreds or thousands—just a few dollars stood between us and the simple freedom to order what we actually wanted to eat.

For some of you reading this, it might be hard to imagine $6 being the difference between constraint and freedom. But at that moment, watching my wife pretend to deliberate over a menu when we both knew exactly what we'd order, it became crystal clear: This wasn't just about dinner choices. This was about living life on someone else's terms, letting our financial limitations box us into corners we never meant to occupy.

Right there, between sips of ice water and bites of the cheapest meal on the menu, I made a decision. I wasn't going to wait for a promotion, hope for a bonus, or pray for a lottery win. I was going to take control of our financial future, even if it meant building it a few dollars at a time. I wanted our next dinner out to be one where we ordered what we truly wanted, where we could focus on our conversation instead of the prices, and where we could leave without that knot of guilt in our stomachs over spending an extra few dollars.

That decision—that moment of clarity in a modest local restaurant—became the catalyst for my journey into the world of side hustles.

The Swiss Army Knife of Income Streams

Now, before you start imagining some get-rich-quick scheme or a second full-time job that'll have you burning the candle at both ends, let's break down what a side hustle really is.

A side hustle is like the Swiss Army knife of income streams. It's versatile, adaptable, and can come in handy when you least expect it. It's not about working yourself to the bone. It's about finding creative ways to supplement your income by doing things you enjoy or are good at.

A Smorgasbord of Opportunities

I didn't just dip my toes into the side hustle waters; I dove in headfirst. Here's a taste of the side hustle buffet I sampled:

- Hot dog vendor at the racetrack (Because nothing says "side hustle" like asking, "Mustard or ketchup?")
- Dish clearer in speedway suites (Proving that sometimes, the fast lane is all about fast cleanup)
- Online reseller (Turning "one man's trash" into "this man's treasure")
- Calligraphy artist (Because even in the digital age, fancy handwriting can pay the bills)

The point is side hustles come in all shapes and sizes. It's not about finding the perfect gig right off the bat. It's about being willing to try new things and see what sticks.

When a Side Hustle Becomes a Main Squeeze

Now, here's where my story takes an interesting turn. Among all these side hustles, I stumbled upon YouTube. At first, it was just a platform to share reviews and helpful tips. Little did I know that this particular side hustle would eventually outgrow my day job.

What did I learn? Sometimes, your side hustle has the potential to become your main squeeze. It might start as a trickle, but with patience and persistence, it can turn into a river of opportunity.

From Pocket Change to Empire Building

Here's the beauty of side hustles: They're not one-size-fits-all. They exist on a spectrum, ranging from "nice little bonus" to "holy cow, I can quit my day job!"

Let's look at some real-world examples from some of my friends:

- **The Candle Queen**: Started making candles in the back of a shop, now runs a full-time candle empire.
- **The Doggy Daycare Dynamo**: Walks and boards dogs during holidays, raking in an extra $30,000 a year.
- **The Wordsmith Wonder**: Writes children's books for school districts, earning thousands each week.
- **The Wedding Invitation Wizard**: Creates custom invitations from home, making hundreds per project.
- **The Melodic Moonlighter**: Plays guitar and sings at local venues in the evenings.

These stories prove that side hustles can be as big or small as you want them to be. It's all about finding what works for you and your lifestyle.

The Secret Sauce

Now, here's the real secret to side hustle success: Start with something you're already interested in or passionate about. When you build on existing skills or interests, it feels less like work and more like, well, fun!

Remember, Rome wasn't built in a day, and neither will your side hustle empire be. The key is to start small, be consistent, and let it grow organically. Who knows? Your little side project might just be the next Apple, FedEx, or Spanx (all started as side hustles)!

The Freedom Factor

Here's a plot twist for you. Side hustles aren't just about padding your bank account. They're about freedom. Financial freedom, sure, but also the freedom to make choices based on what you want, not what you need.

Imagine having a little "freedom fund" each month – an extra $100 or $200 that you can spend however you like. Movie night with the family? Check. Saving for that dream vacation? You got it. Want to buy a classic Mustang convertible? You're on your way. Building a retirement nest egg? Go for it!

The 40-Hour Fallacy

Now, I know what you're thinking: "I barely have time to binge-watch my favorite shows, let alone start a side hustle!" But here's the thing. You don't need to add another full-time job to your plate.

Think of side hustles as the tapas of the working world. You can sample a little bit here and there without committing to a full five-course meal. Even an hour a week can make a difference. Remember, an extra $50 a month might seem small, but it's $50 more than you had before!

The Side Hustle Mindset

As you embark on your side hustle adventure, keep these nuggets of wisdom in mind:

1. **Experiment freely**: Try different things until you find your groove.
2. **Start small**: Even a few hours a week can make a difference.
3. **Follow your interests**: The best side hustles don't feel like work.
4. **Be patient**: Success rarely happens overnight.
5. **Stay flexible**: Be ready to pivot or evolve as you learn.
6. **Enjoy the ride**: It's not just about the destination; it's about the journey.

Your Side Hustle, Your Rules

In the end, your side hustle journey is uniquely yours. Whether you're sweeping construction sites for some peaceful alone time or building the next social media empire, the power is in your hands to create your own stream of easy money.

Remember, a side hustle isn't just a way to make extra cash (although that's why most of us get into it). It's a way to tap into your creativity, explore new passions, and create a safety net that gives you peace of mind in an unpredictable world. It's about transforming your skills and interests into easy money - income that doesn't feel like a grind because you're doing what you love.

I can personally attest to the life-changing power of side hustles. My own side hustle journey catapulted me forward both financially and emotionally. It helped me achieve milestones I once thought impossible, like spending months traveling or buying my dream cars. But here's the crucial point: side hustles don't have to make a fortune to change your life. Even modest earnings can be transformative, especially for those living paycheck to paycheck.

Imagine what an extra $100 or $200 a month could mean. For many households, it's the difference between constant financial stress and having a small but crucial safety net. It could mean finally having an emergency fund or being able to throw a proper birthday party for your child instead of making excuses. That little extra might allow you to fill up your gas tank without anxiety, enabling a family day trip that creates lasting memories. It could mean buying healthier groceries and improving your family's nutrition and well-being. Or perhaps it's the ticket to a stress-free date night, offering a much-needed break from day-to-day pressures.

These may seem like small things, but they can be truly life-altering. They represent breathing room, reduced stress, and moments of joy that might otherwise be out of reach. My side hustles allowed me opportunities and experiences I never expected. But even before reaching that point, the small wins along the way were incredibly impactful. The beauty of it all? These modest earnings can snowball into significant impacts over time, just as they did for me. Remember, financial freedom isn't always about making millions – sometimes, it's about those small, consistent gains that add up to a dramatically improved quality of life.

So, what are you waiting for? Your easy money adventure awaits. That little project you start today might just be the key to unlocking a whole new world of financial possibilities tomorrow. Now, go out there and hustle, but most importantly, have fun doing it! After all, that's what makes it easy money – when work doesn't feel like work at all.

4

Waste Not

Mastering the Art of Interstitial Time

I could feel my brain cells dying, one by one.

Perched on a cold mall bench outside yet another clothing store, I watched the seconds tick by on my phone with the kind of intensity usually reserved for bomb disposal experts. My wife had disappeared inside with those dreaded words every husband knows too well: "I'll just be a few minutes!"

The mall buzzed around me—a cacophony of chattering teenagers, crying babies, and the generic pop music that seemed to follow you from store to store. Hundreds of people streamed past, each lost in their own shopping adventure. But for me, time had slowed to a cruel crawl. I shifted uncomfortably on the bench, already imagining all the productive things I could be doing at home on my computer.

That's when it hit me—a revelation so obvious it was almost embarrassing. Here I was, a grown man, literally counting seconds while my brain turned to mush. Why was I treating this time like a prison sentence? The real waste wasn't the minutes ticking by; it was my acceptance of them as nothing more than a void to be endured.

I sat up straighter, a new thought taking shape. What if these "dead" moments weren't really dead at all? What if my perspective was what needed changing, not the situation? Sure, I couldn't leave my post as the obedient husband, but maybe I didn't have to leave my brain at the entrance either.

Little did I know that this moment of clarity—born from pure, mind-numbing boredom—would lead to a realization that would revolutionize not just my shopping companion duties but my entire approach to time and personal growth.

You've probably heard the phrase, "Reduce, reuse, recycle." Well, it's even more powerful when it comes to your time! Welcome to the world of interstitial time, where waste becomes wisdom, and those seemingly throwaway moments in your day transform into golden opportunities for personal growth. I'm about to turn your time trash into a major boost to improving yourself!

Interstitial Time

Now, before you start wondering if "interstitial" is some sort of complex mechanism, let me break it down for you. Interstitial time is just a fancy way of saying "the space between events." It's those seemingly insignificant pockets of time scattered throughout your day that you probably didn't even realize existed.

- The 30-minute commute to work
- Waiting in line for your morning coffee
- That awkward 10 minutes before a meeting starts
- The time spent folding laundry or doing dishes
- Walking the dog or pushing a stroller

These moments might seem too short or too scattered to be useful, but trust me, they're the secret ingredients to your personal growth smoothie!

From Wasted Minutes to Wisdom

Let me introduce you to my friend Bjorn. Bjorn was your typical busy bee, supporting a family of six and feeling like he barely had time to scratch his nose, let alone read a book. Sound familiar?

One day, I reintroduced Bjorn to the magical world of audiobooks (of course, he knew what they were but hadn't thought about them in ages). Fast forward six months, and guess what? Bjorn had devoured 50 books! That's more books than most people read in years, and he did it all during his "wasted" time.

The lesson here? Your interstitial time is like loose change falling between your couch cushions. It might not seem like much at first, but collect it consistently, and before you know it, you've got enough for a tropical vacation! (Okay, maybe not a tropical vacation, but definitely enough for a Shamrock shake, which also brings me a crazy amount of joy.)

Small Tools with Big Impacts

Now that we've established that interstitial time is the unsung hero of personal development, let's talk about how to harness its power. Here are some tools to add to your interstitial arsenal:

1. **Audiobooks**: Services like Audible or Libby (for free library audiobooks) are your new best friends. Pro tip: Listen at 1.5x or 2x speed to turbocharge your learning!
2. **Podcasts**: There's a podcast for every interest under the sun. Whether you're into true crime, business strategies, or the mating habits of sea animals, there's something for you.
3. **Educational YouTube Videos**: Who says YouTube is just for cat videos? Subscribe to channels that align with your interests or career goals.
4. **Mobile Note-Taking Apps**: Tools like Evernote or Apple Notes sync across all your devices. Capture that brilliant idea while waiting for your coffee – because let's let's be honest, genius doesn't wait for a convenient time!

5. **Micro-Learning Platforms**: Platforms like Blinkist or GetAbstract condense big ideas into bite-sized chunks. Perfect for when you're waiting at the dentist (and need a distraction anyway).

6. **Digital Flashcard Apps**: Tools like Anki or Quizlet are perfect for reinforcing knowledge in short bursts. Whether you're studying for a certification or learning industry terms, these are your pocket-sized teachers.

7. **Digital Reading Apps**: Pocket or Instapaper lets you save interesting articles to read later. Turn your commute into a personal growth session – way better than doom-scrolling social media!

8. **Voice Recording Apps**: Tools like Otter.ai or Rev let you capture thoughts on the go. Because sometimes, your best ideas show up when your hands are full of groceries!

9. **Project Writing Apps**: Keep Google Docs on your phone and turn those random moments into book-writing progress. That plot twist that hits you in the checkout line? Captured. That perfect chapter opening while waiting for your kid's practice to end? Done. Because your next bestseller is built in these stolen moments!

10. **Course Creation Tools**: Transform your expertise into an online course, one tiny step at a time. Pull up your course outline during those "in-between" moments and flesh out module ideas, add examples, or brainstorm exercises. Tools like Trello or Notion make it easy to organize your thoughts on the go.

11. **Social Media Design Apps**: Turn waiting time into creating time with Canva on your phone. Share your journey, design quick quote cards, or craft mini-carousel posts showcasing your latest insights. Because building your personal brand doesn't need a four-hour block – sometimes a few free minutes is all it takes!

12. **Relationship Building Tools**: Keep a "Connections List" in your favorite notes app. Waiting for your coffee to brew? Perfect time to send that "thinking of you" text or record a quick video message to brighten someone's day. Use apps like BombBomb or Loom to make personal connections in seconds.

13. **Content Calendar Apps**: Use tools like Airtable or Asana to map out your

content strategy. Those five minutes before a Zoom call? That's enough time to schedule your next week of posts or brainstorm content themes.

Turning "Ugh" into "Aha!"

Now, I know what you're thinking. "Pete, this sounds great and all, but I barely have the energy to think about what I'm having for dinner, let alone tackle quantum physics during my commute."

Relax! The beauty of the interstitial approach is that it's all about baby steps and following your interests. Here's how to shift your mindset:

1. **Start Small**: Begin with just a few minutes a day. That's less time than it takes to decide what to watch on Netflix!
2. **Follow Your Passion**: Choose topics that genuinely excite you. Pick what you want to consume, not what you think you should consume. Learning should be fun, not a chore.
3. **Mix It Up**: Some days, I'm just not up for another podcast episode, and I just want to retreat to 80s Rock. Alternate between educational content and pure entertainment. Balance is key!
4. **Celebrate Small Wins**: Finished a chapter? Learned a new word in Spanish? Do a little victory dance! High-five a stranger! Buy yourself an ice cream.

And here's something crucial I want you to understand: while we've talked a lot about learning during these moments, interstitial time isn't just about consuming information—it's about creating too.

Take it from someone who knows. I've written several books, and interstitial time has been my secret weapon. Imagine working on your own book, course, or guide. Every time you have a few spare moments, you whip out your phone, pull up your document, and add a few ideas. Maybe it's just a sentence or two. Perhaps it's a whole paragraph if inspiration strikes.

Those five-minute writing spurts might seem insignificant in the moment, but do the math—by the end of the month, you've carved out over two and a half hours of creative time. That's a massive advantage over someone who's still in the "planning phase," waiting for that mythical perfect time to start. Before you know it, a month or two has passed, and you're staring at a completed project that materialized in the cracks of your busy life.

But here's the beautiful thing—it doesn't have to be about finishing a project or professional development at all. These moments can be portals to joy and connection in your everyday life. Maybe you use that five-minute wait at the doctor's office to research a fun, budget-friendly weekend activity for your family. While waiting for your coffee to brew, you might discover a hidden gem of a restaurant for date night. Those few minutes before a meeting starts? Perfect time to browse local events and find that movie in the park you can invite friends to.

Or better yet, use these moments to nurture your relationships. Fire off a quick email to that college friend you've been meaning to catch up with. Send a text to your buddy from high school. These small actions might seem trivial, but they're the building blocks of lasting connections. Over time, these tiny investments in relationships compound into a richer, more connected life.

This is where the concept of microlearning comes into play perfectly. Microlearning is the practice of breaking down complex subjects into bite-sized, easily digestible chunks of information. It's tailor-made for our fast-paced, attention-challenged world – and it meshes beautifully with interstitial time.

Think about it. Those 5-10 minute pockets of time are ideal for consuming a single, focused lesson or concept. Whether it's a quick language lesson, a bite-sized history fact, or a compact coding tutorial, microlearning allows you to make meaningful progress in short bursts. This approach not only fits seamlessly into your interstitial moments but also aligns with how our brains naturally process and retain information.

By combining interstitial time with microlearning, you're not just making use of spare moments – you're optimizing your learning efficiency. It's like killing two birds with one stone. You're utilizing time that would otherwise be wasted, and you're learning in a way that maximizes retention and understanding. So the next time you find yourself with a few minutes to spare, remember: you're not just killing time. You're engaging in a powerful form of learning that's perfectly suited to our modern lives.

Watch Your Knowledge Grow!

Here's the coolest part about leveraging your interstitial time. It creates a snowball effect. The more you learn, the more you want to learn. Suddenly, you're looking forward to that traffic jam because it means extra time with your favorite podcast. You're volunteering to walk the dog because it's your chance to finish that audiobook chapter.

Before you know it, you're dropping random facts at dinner parties, impressing your boss with innovative ideas, and maybe even contemplating that career change you've always dreamed about. All because you decided to make friends with your "wasted" time!

The Interstitial Hall of Fame

Ready to dive into the world of interstitial learning but not sure where to start? Here's a curated list of podcasts that I love to kick-start your journey:

- **For the Curious Minds**: "Freakonomics" and "Stuff You Should Know" Perfect for: Those who love asking "Why?" and aren't afraid of diving into random topics.
- **For the Aspiring Moguls**: "Business Wars" and "The Side Hustle Show" Perfect for: Entrepreneurs and anyone looking to add a comma to their bank account.
- **For the Number Crunchers**: "CNBC's Fast Money" and "ChooseFI" Perfect for: Finance enthusiasts and those who want to make their money work harder than they do.
- **For the Sports Nuts**: "The Pat McAfee Show" and "Locked On [Your Favorite Team]" Perfect for: Those who treat fantasy sports like a second job.
- **For the Science Geeks**: "Science Friday" Perfect for: Anyone who's ever

wondered how to build a lightsaber (and other, you know, actual scientific stuff).

- **For the News Junkies**: "WSJ What's News" and "Breaking Points with Krystal and Saagar" Perfect for: Staying informed without mindless scrolling through social media.
- **For the Laugh Seekers**: "Conan O'Brien Needs a Friend" and "The Way I Heard It with Mike Rowe" Perfect for: Those who believe laughter is the best medicine (and procrastination tool).

Your Time, Your Rules

Remember, the goal here isn't to turn every second of your day into a productivity marathon. Sometimes, you need to zone out, listen to your favorite playlist, or just enjoy the silence. The beauty of mastering your interstitial time is that it's entirely up to you how you use it.

Remember Bjorn? The guy who went from reading no books to devouring 50 every six months? Imagine how much more informed, inspired, and equipped a person is who's read one meaningful book versus someone who hasn't read one at all. Now imagine that person has read two, three, fifty, or 100 more books. Can you see how much more powerful and resourceful that person could be? Just by using their interstitial time to do short bursts of learning? The impact is immeasurable and very real.

By recognizing and harnessing these pockets of time, you're not just becoming more efficient – you're opening doors to new passions, skills, and opportunities. You're turning what was once wasted time into wisdom, transforming idle moments into intellectual gold. Who knows? That podcast you listen to while doing the dishes might just spark the idea for your next big adventure, or that book you read in short bursts while waiting in line could completely change your perspective on life.

So, the next time you find yourself waiting in line, stuck in traffic, or folding your umpteenth shirt of the day, remember: you're not just killing time. You're alchemizing it. You're converting waste into wisdom. And that can help you take a giant leap ahead.

5

The Cheat Code

Welcome To Reality

Nineteen thousand dollars.

I stared at the check in my hands, trying to make sense of the number. Fifteen years of homeownership, condensed into this single piece of paper. The closing agent had already left, leaving my wife and me alone in the conference room, both of us silent as the reality sank in.

This was it. This was what we had to show for our first home—a condo we'd bought before we even said "I do," where we'd spent our first decade of marriage, and that we'd later transformed into a rental property. Nineteen thousand dollars. It felt like a cruel joke.

We'd done everything "right." We'd bought within our means. We'd rounded up our monthly payments, throwing extra money at the mortgage whenever we could. We'd even managed to keep it as a rental property when we moved to our dream home, letting our tenant's payments chip away at the loan balance. And when the stars aligned—housing prices up, interest rates down—we'd sold it.

By all conventional wisdom, we should have been sitting pretty. After fifteen years—half the life of a standard mortgage—shouldn't we have owned half the home? The math should have worked in our favor. Instead, we were holding a check that felt more like a participation trophy than a reward for fifteen years of responsible homeownership.

That's when it hit me: We'd been playing the game all wrong. We'd followed all the rules and made all the "smart" moves, and yet here we were, with barely enough equity to buy a decent used car. If this was how the traditional mortgage game worked, there had to be a better way to play it.

As my wife and I drove home that day, my mind was already racing. Our new house, our dream home, came with its own 30-year mortgage—a fresh mountain to climb. But this time would be different. This time, we weren't going to spend decades barely scratching the surface of true ownership. This time, we were going to change the rules.

I'm about to dive into the ultimate debt cheat code - a financial hack so powerful that it'll make you feel like you've just been given administrator privileges to your mortgage. Welcome to the world of equity optimization, where I'll show you how to pay off your 30-year mortgage in record time!

A 30-Year Nightmare?

Ah, the American Dream. White picket fence, 2.5 kids, and a mortgage that'll outlive your career. Wait, what? That's right. Somewhere along the line, the American Dream became less about financial independence and more about signing up for a 30-year commitment to your friendly neighborhood bank.

Now, don't get me wrong. Homeownership is great. But what if I told you there's a way to have your cake and eat it too? What if you could own your home outright in just 5-6 years without living on ramen noodles or having to imagine life without your internal organs? Intrigued? Then, let's dive into the magical world of equity optimization!

Where Your Money Gets Lost

Before we jump into our financial DeLorean and speed towards a mortgage-free future, let's break down what a mortgage actually is. (Don't worry. I promise this won't be as boring as watching paint dry.)

Imagine your mortgage as a giant pizza. When you first start paying, most of your payment is just the cheese (interest), with only a tiny sliver of pepperoni (principal) on top. As time goes on, you get more and more pepperoni, but it takes forever to get to the good stuff!

For example:

- Your monthly payment: $1,000
- Amount going to interest (cheese): $900
- Amount going to principal (pepperoni): $100

This is why making extra payments can be so powerful. It's like getting extra pepperoni right from the start!

The Equity Optimization Revolution

Now, what if I told you there's a way to hack this system? A way to pay off your mortgage faster without changing your lifestyle or eating nothing but rice and beans for the next decade? Enter: Equity Optimization.

This strategy is like finding a secret wormhole in the Delta quadrant. It gets you to the end of the journey way faster, and you don't have to be a financial wizard to use it. Here's how it works:

1. **Understand the Power of Principal**: Remember our pizza analogy? By paying extra towards the principal early on, you're essentially skipping ahead in the game. If you pay an extra $500, you could be knocking out five future payments in one go!
2. **Harness the HELOC**: This is where things get interesting. A Home Equity Line of Credit (HELOC) gives you flexible access to cash. It allows you to borrow against your home's equity and pay it back as you can.
3. **The Magic Dance**: Use your HELOC to make large principal payments on your mortgage, then use your regular income to pay off the balance of the HELOC. Rinse and repeat. It's like a beautiful waltz, except instead of impressing your in-laws at a wedding, you're demolishing

your mortgage.

But Wait, There's More!

Now, again, I know what you're thinking. "Pete, this sounds great, but I don't have thousands of dollars lying around to throw at my mortgage!" Don't worry. This is where the HELOC really shines.

Think of a HELOC as a giant piggy bank attached to your house. You can take money out when you need it and put it back when you can. Unlike your mortgage, which only accepts payments in one direction, a HELOC is bi-directional.

Here's how you can use it to your advantage:

1. Open a HELOC
2. Use the HELOC to make a large payment on your mortgage principal
3. Use your regular income to pay off the HELOC
4. Borrow from the HELOC to cover your normal living expenses
5. Once the HELOC is completely paid off, do it again!

Basically, you are using short-term loans from the HELOC to leapfrog ahead in your mortgage payments. It may take you a few months to pay off the HELOC, but it could mean lopping off years of your mortgage.

"Sounds Too Good to Be True!"

Now, I get it. When I first heard about this strategy, I was more skeptical than a Trojan being offered a horse. It seemed too good to be true like those ads promising to make you a millionaire by working from home in your pajamas.

But here's the thing. It works. And it's not magic. It's math. Although to be fair, sometimes math feels like magic.

The key is understanding that by making large principal payments early, you're not just reducing your balance – you're skipping ahead in time. You're telling your mortgage, "Hey, I know we just met, but I'm ready to commit.

Let's skip the first few years of payments!"

Financial Freedom, Here We Come!

Imagine a life without a mortgage payment. No, really. Close your eyes and picture it. What would you do with all that extra money each month? Travel the world? Start a business? Buy your dream car? Retire?

With the equity optimization strategy, this dream can become a reality much sooner than you think. We're talking 5-6 years instead of 30. That's like going from the Stone Age to SpaceX in terms of financial progress!

Here's a quick recap of why this strategy is the bee's knees:

1. Pay off your mortgage in 5-6 years (instead of 30)
2. No lifestyle changes required (keep your date nights)
3. Maintain financial flexibility with a HELOC
4. Save thousands in interest payments
5. Achieve the real American Dream: homeownership free and clear

Your Next Steps

If you're ready to kiss your mortgage goodbye and start your journey to financial freedom, here's what you need to do:

1. **Crunch the numbers**: Understand your current mortgage situation
2. **Research HELOCs**: Shop around for the best rates and terms
3. **Make a plan**: Decide how much you can comfortably put toward your HELOC each month
4. **Take action**: Open that HELOC and start the optimization dance!
5. **Celebrate**: Start planning what you'll do with all that extra money once your mortgage is gone!

Look, this is the shortest summary of this strategy I could put together. I have an entire course and book that details the ins and outs for those who want to get a strong grasp of the concepts and details. But if the idea of being mortgage-free is enticing, here's the real kicker. This strategy isn't just about mortgages. It's a financial game-changer that can revolutionize your entire debt situation.

Imagine wiping out your biggest debt - your mortgage - in a fraction of the time. But why stop at your mortgage? This equity optimization strategy works on any debt. Got a six-year car loan? How about paying it off in just one year? Credit card debt that's been hanging over your head? Picture it gone in a matter of months.

The possibilities are mind-boggling. Imagine your life completely free of all debts - no mortgage, no car payments, no credit card bills. It's not a far-off dream; it's a reality that's much closer and more achievable than you might think.

This strategy isn't about living like a hermit or sacrificing your quality of life. It's about being smarter with the money you already have. It's like discovering a financial cheat code that works on every level of the game.

So, are you ready to apply this debt cheat code and supercharge your path to total financial freedom? Are you prepared to laugh in the face of long-term debts and watch them disappear faster than you ever thought possible? Then let's do this! There is a life available with options and opportunities you never imagined if you master this ultimate financial strategy.

Welcome to the world of equity optimization, your newfound path to financial liberation. With this knowledge, you're no longer just playing defense against debt - you're on the offensive, armed with a powerful strategy to eliminate it entirely. Your debts don't stand a chance against your financial wizardry. It's time to reclaim your financial future and experience the true game-changing power of being completely debt-free.

6

Time Recovery

The Only True Time Hack

The clock on my desk read 1:47 AM. Again.

My toddler would be up in four hours, ready to start his day with the boundless energy only a two-year-old can muster. My presentation for work was due at 9 AM, and my YouTube channel's content schedule was already a week behind. The coffee beside me had gone cold hours ago, but I took another sip anyway, grimacing at both the taste and the realization that this had become my new normal.

Something had to give.

On paper, everything looked manageable. A decent career in financial services—demanding but not crushing. A growing side hustle that was actually making money. A beautiful family that brought meaning to it all. But in reality, I was juggling chainsaws while riding a unicycle on a tightrope, and my arms were getting tired.

Every day felt like a cruel game of Whac-A-Mole. Rush to get my son to school, sprint through a full workday, make dinner, squeeze in family time, and then burn the midnight oil on my side hustle. Sleep? That was becoming more of a fond memory than a daily reality.

The conventional wisdom screamed at me from every direction: "Pick one lane!" "You can't have it all!" "Something has to go!" The choices seemed brutally binary—abandon my growing side hustle or quit my stable career. Both options felt like admitting defeat, like cutting off a limb to save the body.

If I focused solely on my side hustle, there was no guarantee it would survive, let alone thrive. (After all, it was run by a moron.) But if I abandoned my career path in financial services, I'd be walking away from years of building something secure. And if I dropped the side hustle only to later lose my job? Well, that scenario kept me up at night even more than my current schedule did.

I kept running the numbers, trying to find a way out. Hiring help seemed like the obvious answer—it's what every successful entrepreneur preached. But at $19 an hour minimum wage in my area, the math was laughable. I'd essentially be working my day job just to pay someone else to run my side hustle. It felt like being stuck in a financial escape room where none of the clues added up.

Then, at my lowest point, when I was seriously considering whether humans actually needed sleep to survive, I stumbled upon a revelation that would change everything—a solution so obvious yet revolutionary that it felt like discovering a secret club.

We're talking about the only true time hack in the business world. Forget your productivity apps and your time management gurus. The real key to bending time to your will? Overseas virtual assistants. I'm about to turn your 24-hour day into what feels like a 48-hour powerhouse of productivity!

A Cautionary Tale

Imagine that you're an eager and optimistic entrepreneur ready to conquer the world. You've got dreams bigger than your coffee mug (and let's face it, that thing's practically a bucket). Then, some "wise" mentor comes along and drops this gem on you:

"Want to succeed? Simple! Just hire an office professional for $60,000 a year. Oh, and don't forget benefits and taxes. Now, go make it rain!"

Excuse me, what? That's like telling a toddler to run a marathon before they've mastered walking. It's the kind of advice that makes you wonder if your mentor's been sipping a little too much of the success Kool-Aid.

But don't worry! There's an easy way to scale your business. Enter the world of overseas virtual assistants – your ticket to freedom, growth, and maybe even a social life.

Not Just for Scheduling Cat Videos

Now, when I say "virtual assistant," I don't mean Siri's more competent cousin. I'm talking about real, talented professionals who can help you scale your business faster than you can say "outsourcing."

These aren't just folks who schedule your meetings and remind you to buy milk. Oh no, we're talking about skilled professionals who can edit videos, manage your social media, handle customer service, and maybe even run your entire business better than you.

The Philippines

While you can find virtual assistants from all over the world, the Philippines has some distinct advantages that make it my preferred place for outsourcing. Here's why:

1. **English Proficiency**: English is an official language in the Philippines. So unless you're planning to communicate exclusively in interpretive dance, you're golden.
2. **Cultural Compatibility**: Filipino culture values hard work, loyalty, respect, and adaptability. It's like they were custom-made for awesome working relationships!
3. **Cost-Effectiveness**: Your dollar stretches further here than you could ever imagine. One of my virtual assistants started at just $1 per hour.
4. **Tech-Savvy Workforce**: Internet access is widespread, and many Filipinos are well-versed in the latest digital tools

How to Hire Your Philippine Dream Team

Ready to dip your toes into the virtual assistant pool? Here's your step-by-step guide to hiring success:

1. **Define Your Needs**: What tasks are eating up your time? Video editing? Customer service? Reminding you to wear pants for Zoom calls?
2. **Set Your Budget**: For skilled roles like video editing, expect to pay between $400-$1000 per month. Remember, in the Philippines, this is considered a good to incredible salary.
3. **Post Your Job**: Use platforms like onlinejobs.ph and virtualstaff.ph to find your perfect match. It's like online dating but for your business!
4. **Interview and Test**: Email potential hires and give them a test project. Make sure they're a good fit for your business (and your sense of humor).
5. **Seal the Deal**: Once you've found your virtual soulmate, agree on terms and get ready for business magic to happen!

Payments, Taxes, and Other Fun Stuff

Now, let's talk about the less exciting (but super important) bits:

- **Payment**: Weekly pay is standard. Use services like Wise.com to transfer funds directly to your VA's GCash wallet. It's fast and my workers prefer it.
- **Taxes and Benefits**: Here's the beautiful part – your overseas VA is considered an independent contractor. That means no unemployment taxes or benefits to worry about. (But remember, being a decent human being and treating your VA well is always good business practice!)
- **13th Month**: Unlike local employees, independent contractors/VAs aren't legally entitled to 13th month pay (one month of additional salary paid in December). However, many employers choose to give year-end bonuses as a gesture of appreciation and to keep workers from be lured away by local jobs.

- **Communication**: Email, chat, video calls (although my team doesn't like them) – whatever works for you. Just remember, clear communication is key to a successful working relationship.

The Unexpected Perks

Sure, hiring a VA will help you scale your business. But the real magic happens when you least expect it. Here are some surprising benefits:

1. **Time Freedom**: Suddenly, you're not chained to your desk 24/7. You might even remember what sunlight looks like!
2. **Creativity Boost**: With the boring tasks off your plate, your brain is free to come up with the next big idea. Who knows, you might invent the next disruptive business.
3. **Life Balance**: Remember hobbies? Family? Friends? Yeah, you can have those again.
4. **Business Growth**: With a team handling the day-to-day, you're free to focus on big-picture strategies. World domination, here we come!
5. **Better Results**: Often, your VA brings skills you don't have. My VAs run circles around me with social media and SEO – they've done it for years and know all the tricks. Sometimes, letting go means watching your business soar higher than you could take it alone.
6. **Happiness**: Turns out, not working yourself to the bone can actually make you... happy. Who knew?

My VA Victory Story

Let me get personal for a moment. Before I hired my VA team, creating YouTube videos was sucking the life out of me faster than a bird-sized mosquito. I was spending my entire week filming and editing, and by Friday, I couldn't stand the sound of my own voice.

But then, I took the plunge and hired a talented video editor from the Philippines. Suddenly, I went from spending 40 hours a week on content creation to just a few hours of filming. The result? Not only did my content quality improve, but I also rediscovered this weird thing called "free time."

This summer, instead of being glued to my computer, I was out making memories with my family. We traveled, we laughed, we lived. And you know what? My business didn't just survive – it thrived.

Work Smarter, Not Harder

Look, I get it. The idea of hiring someone overseas might seem scary. What if there are communication issues? What if the quality isn't up to par? What if they secretly replace all your video content with cat memes? (Okay, that last one might actually make you rich.)

But here's the reality. Hiring a virtual assistant isn't just about offloading work. It's about reclaiming your life. It's about remembering why you started your business in the first place – probably not so you could work 80-hour weeks and forget what your family looks like.

So, are you ready to embrace the only true time hack in the entrepreneurial playbook? Ready to scale your business, rediscover your passion, and maybe even take a vacation that doesn't involve checking your email every five minutes?

Remember, life's too short to do it all yourself. Delegate, automate, and take a break once in a while. Your business (and your mental health) will thank you.

Welcome to the world of virtual assistants - the only true time hack you'll ever need. It's not just about managing your time; it's about multiplying it. With this strategy, you're not just working with the hours in a day - you're transcending them. You're creating a business that runs smoothly while you sleep, while you vacation, and while you dream up your next big idea.

This isn't just a productivity tip; it's a complete paradigm shift. It's the closest thing to cloning yourself or bending the laws of physics to create more time. So go ahead and take the plunge into the virtual assistant revolution. A time-rich life awaits!

7

Living The Dream!

Dealing Your Way to a Better Life

Alright, we've reached the final table of our life-changing poker game. I've dealt you five incredible cards, each one a strategy that can transform your life. Now, it's time to see how these cards come together to create a hand so powerful that it'll make even Lady Luck do a double-take.

The Five-Card Draw That'll Change Your Game

Let's recap our winning hand.

1. **The Ace of Organization**: Freeing up time while being more productive and accurate
2. **The Two of Cash Flow**: Generating extra cash for new opportunities
3. **The Three of Interstitial Time**: Capitalizing on those sneaky pockets of free time
4. **The Four of Freedom**: Bulldoze your debt and mortgage
5. **The Five of Delegation**: Offloading tasks to reclaim your life

Now, each of these cards is pretty nifty on its own. But stack 'em together?

You've got yourself a nearly unbeatable hand of life improvement!

When Good Things Snowball

Here's the beautiful thing about these strategies. They're like those fancy domino setups that spell out "AWESOME LIFE" in giant, colorful letters.

Start by getting organized, and suddenly, you've got time for a side hustle. That side hustle starts generating extra cash, which you can throw at your mortgage, your debts, your retirement, or your dreams. All the while, you're maximizing those sneaky pockets of free time, becoming skilled and more promotable by the minute.

And just when you think it can't get any better, you delegate those pesky, time-sucking tasks, freeing yourself up to live your best life and chase your dreams like they owe you money.

The result? A life so fulfilling, productive, and financially secure, it'll make you wonder if you should've been on the cover of Fortune Magazine.

The Universal Cheat Code

Now, I can hear you say it. "Pete, this sounds great and all, but I'm just a regular Joe/Jane. Can this really work for me?"

Well, let me tell you a little secret. These strategies are like that one-size-fits-all hat at the gift shop – they actually do fit all! Whether you're a fresh-faced college grad, a mid-career professional wondering where all the time went, or someone who's been around the block so many times you've worn a groove in the sidewalk, these strategies can work for you.

Maybe you can't implement all five strategies at once. That's okay! Rome wasn't built in a day, and your dream life won't be either. Start with one. Get organized. Or start maximizing that interstitial time. It's like planting a seed – nurture it, and before you know it, you'll have a whole garden of new opportunities growing in your life.

The Long Game

Here's the thing about these strategies – they're not overnight success promises or magical life hacks. They're more like the financial equivalent of a slow cooker: set it, forget it, and watch as something amazing develops.

These strategies might be the difference between:

- Working until you're the oldest person at your company vs. retiring early enough to actually enjoy it
- Choosing between a demanding career and quality time with your family (spoiler alert: with these strategies, you might not have to choose!)
- Just getting by vs. getting ahead and doing things you never thought possible

Your Personal Roadmap to Awesome

Think of this book as your personal GPS to a better life. Sure, you could probably figure out the route on your own, but why take the scenic route when you can race straight to the summit?

I discovered these strategies the hard way, stumbling around in the dark for years. But you? You've got the cheat codes. Use them!

Your Move

So, here we are at the end of our journey. I've dealt you a winning hand – five strategies that, when played right, can transform your life from a game of Uno to a Vegas-worthy poker championship. But this isn't just about winning a game; it's about truly living the dream.

These strategies have the power to break you out of the daily grind, to stop you from merely existing, and to start truly living. They can help you pursue your passions, build your dream business, achieve financial independence, and create a life so awesome it belongs on a motivational poster. In short, they're your roadmap to living the dream – your dream, whatever that may be.

Remember, you don't have to be a financial wizard or a time management guru to make these strategies work. They're designed for real people living real lives. All you need is the willingness to try, the patience to let them work their magic, and maybe a tiny bit of that can-do spirit.

So, what are you waiting for? It's time to ante up, play your cards right, and start building the life you've always dreamed of. Now it's your move. The dream life you've always wanted isn't just a fantasy anymore; it's a tangible goal within your reach.

Are you ready to go all in on your awesome future? Are you prepared to transform your life from the daily grind to living the dream? Whether your dream is financial freedom, more time with family, pursuing a passion project, or simply having the flexibility to say "yes" to life's adventures, these strategies are your toolkit for making it happen. You're not just playing the game of life anymore; you're rewriting the rules in your favor.

So take these strategies, make them your own, and watch as your life transforms from the every day to the extraordinary. It's time to stop dreaming about the life you want and begin your incredible expedition!

About the Author

Peter Waitzman is the founder and CEO of Expedition Money LLC, an innovative financial wellness accelerator, that delivers a broad spectrum of financial strategies in a fun and engaging style. He is an author, speaker, and financial wellness enthusiast with over two decades of professional experience in personal finance.

You can connect with me on:

🌐 http://www.waitzman.com

Also by Peter Waitzman

I frequently write books about money, sharing my personal journey, experiences, and lessons learned along the way. My goal is to help you shortcut your path to financial independence and happiness by learning from both my successes and mistakes. Through these books, I aim to provide you with practical insights and strategies that can accelerate your own financial growth and overall well-being.

Discovering Travel Bliss: Insider Secrets For Transforming Ordinary Trips Into Joyful Journeys
With insider tips and real-world examples, this book will equip you to create vacations that refresh your spirit, broaden your horizons, and leave you with stories to tell for years.

Rethink Money: Why Common Money Rules Are Holding You Back
Whether you're drowning in debt or sitting on a fortune, this book will revolutionize the way you think about money. It's time to stop following the herd and start building the financial future you really want.

The Accidental YouTuber: How I Make a Six-Figure Income on YouTube

Embark on a journey with Peter as he shares his rollercoaster ride **from orphan to YouTube success**. With a blend of **candid storytelling** and actionable insights, this book unveils the secrets behind creating engaging content, growing a loyal audience, and monetizing your passion on the world's largest video platform.

Just The Essential Disney Hacks: Discounts & Fun From Booking To Visit

This is the ultimate guide for enjoying Disney World on a budget. This book is packed with insider tips, money-saving strategies, and practical advice to help you get the most out of your Disney experience without overspending. Whether you're a first-time visitor or a seasoned Disney fan, you'll discover ways to make your trip magical and affordable.

Be Discovered: How to Market Your Financial Coaching Business

Whether you're just starting out or looking to take your existing coaching practice to the next level, this book will give you the tools, strategies, and inspiration you need to succeed. Don't just be a financial coach – be discovered and **make a lasting difference** in the lives of your clients.

Money Is Factscinating: Fascinating Money Facts, History, Stories & Trivia

Dive into the captivating world of money with a treasure trove of more than **100 entertaining, informative, and educational stories** that explore the many facets of currency. From mind-blowing tales and historical anecdotes to hilarious mishaps and cutting-edge financial technology, this book offers a fresh and engaging perspective on the subject that makes the world go round.

Amazing Money Stories: True Tales of Greed, Generosity, Success & Luck

Discover a treasure trove of astonishing true stories about money. This captivating collection unveils the incredible ways people have amassed fortunes, realized their wildest dreams, pulled off audacious scams, and uncovered mind-boggling facts about wealth.

How To Get Out Of Debt Fast: Scratch, Claw, Strategize, & Shortcut

Getting out of debt does not have to mean a lifetime of sacrifices. Your journey could be shorter than you think. If you're ready to make the expedition to freedom as fast as possible, then start here.

Vacations Are A Need: How To Make Extraordinary Memories Affordable

This is your ultimate guide to finding a refreshing trip while keeping your budget intact. This comprehensive resource is packed with ingenious travel hacks, insider tips, and practical advice to ensure you can enjoy extraordinary adventures without breaking the bank.

www.ingramcontent.com/pod-product-compliance
Lightning Source LLC
Chambersburg PA
CBHW070137230526
45472CB00004B/1575